D0710016

12 SUPER-SMART ANIMALS
YOU NEED TO KNOW

by Carol Hand

www.12StoryLibrary.com

12-Story Library is an imprint of Peterson Publishing Company and Press Room Editions.

Produced for 12-Story Library by Red Line Editorial

Photographs ©: Rob Hainer/iStockphoto, cover, 1; Csondy/iStockphoto, 4, 28; Ajevs/iStockphoto, 5; knape/iStockphoto, 6; lirtlon/iStockphoto, 7, 29; Michael Price/iStockphoto, 8; Redders48/iStockphoto, 9; Mark R. Higgins/iStockphoto, 10; Liz Leyden/iStockphoto, 11, 27; Damian Kuzdak/iStockphoto, 12; Dennis W. Donohue/Shutterstock Images, 13; Alona Rjabceva/iStockphoto, 14; s5iztok/iStockphoto, 15; Britta Kasholm-Tengve/iStockphoto, 16; Davor Lovincic/iStockphoto, 17; mychadre77/iStockphoto, 18; HNC Photo/Shutterstock Images, 19; technotr/iStockphoto, 20; janecat/iStockphoto, 21; forestc/iStockphoto, 22; Lupico/iStockphoto, 23; MaleWitch/Shutterstock Images, 24; scooperdigital/iStockphoto, 25, 26

ISBN
978-1-63235-141-8 (hardcover)
978-1-63235-183-8 (paperback)
978-1-62143-235-7 (hosted ebook)

Library of Congress Control Number: 2015934279

Printed in the United States of America
Mankato, MN
June, 2015

Go beyond the book. Get free, up-to-date content on this topic at 12StoryLibrary.com.

TABLE OF CONTENTS

AFRICAN GRAY PARROTS CREATE NEW WORDS

Alex, an African gray parrot, could say and understand 150 words. Alex talked with people and used words correctly. He asked for food or toys and said "no" when he did not want to do something. Sometimes he chewed important papers or knocked over a cup. Then he would lower his head and say, "I'm sorry." He told his owner, "You be good. I love you." Alex also made up words. His word for apple was "ban-erry." He thought apples tasted like bananas and looked similar to big cherries.

African gray parrots are one of the smartest known birds. They learn from people and from other parrots. They can name colors and shapes and count corners on objects. They do this as well as some young children. Alex was shown a green cup and a green key. When asked, "What's same?" he said "color." When asked, "What's different?" he said "shape." His answers show that he understood the words. He was not just copying sounds.

Wild African gray parrots make their nests high up in trees.

If an African gray parrot sees an object and someone then covers it, the parrot understands the object is still there. They can watch a person put two types of food into two cups. They remember which cup has each type of food. If a scientist removes the food from one cup, a parrot picks the cup that still has food. These behaviors show intelligence. African gray parrots have excellent memories, so they learn easily. They can learn an amazing amount, partly because

African gray parrots use their beaks to open hard objects, such as nuts.

150

Number of words Alex the African gray parrot could understand.

- Parrots understand words and can speak to people.
- They show the intelligence of a 3.5-year-old child.
- They have excellent memories and learn easily.
- African gray parrots can solve problems.

they live so long. A healthy, happy African gray parrot can live up to 70 years in captivity. They also live in the African tropics and travel in large, noisy flocks.

THINK ABOUT IT

Reread this section about African gray parrots. There are many examples of intelligence. Which examples do you find most interesting? Explain.

ANTS SWARM TO HELP EACH OTHER

Most people think smart animals must have big brains. So how could ants, with their tiny insect brains, be smart? There are 12,000 different kinds of ants on Earth. Ants are social insects. They live together in large colonies, or communities. They depend on each other. Ant colonies can contain thousands to millions of ants. The number of ants varies based on the type of ant and the age of the colony.

Ants divide their work. Different ants do different tasks. Only one is a queen that lays eggs. A few are soldiers that protect the colony. Most are workers that build and repair the nest. They care for the queen and the young. Many go out to look for food. Ants find the shortest path to food over long distances. They communicate and defend their colony against enemies. They care for their larvae, or babies, by feeding and washing them.

Ant colonies can grow to be massive.

Ants use swarm intelligence. In an ant colony, a single ant is not in charge. It communicates by touch and smell. When two ants touch antennae, they smell each other. Every ant has a different scent. When all ants act together as a swarm, their behavior is smart. When an ant locates food, it takes a piece of it home. Along the path, the ant leaves a trail of a pheromone, or body chemical. Other ants follow the trail back to the food, but the smell disappears quickly. At first the ants wander around, but they soon learn the quickest path. As more and more ants follow this path, their pheromones make the trail clearer.

Ants work together to make the colony run smoothly.

5,000
Average number of harvester ants in a colony.

- Ants are social insects and live in colonies.
- They cooperate and care for each other.
- They use swarm intelligence.
- Ants communicate with body chemicals called pheromones.

HUMANS COPY ANT INTELLIGENCE

Humans copy ant swarm intelligence to decide the best routes for trucks. Companies deliver products over long distances. They choose the quickest routes to get the job done. This helps them save time, money, and gas.

BOTTLE-NOSED DOLPHINS WORK TOGETHER

Bottle-nosed dolphins are playful ocean mammals. They surf waves, play tag, and chase each other. They play catch with fish or turtles. In Hawaii, dolphins play with their huge cousins, humpback whales. A dolphin swims onto a whale's nose. The whale raises itself high out of the water, and the dolphin slides down the whale's head and makes a big splash.

Captive dolphins easily learn tricks from their trainers.

Bottle-nosed dolphins learn, teach, and work together. Billie, an injured dolphin,

BRAIN SIZE

Many smart animals have large brains. Scientists compare brain sizes using a measurement called EQ. Smarter animals have larger EQs. Dolphin EQs are second only to human EQs. The human's EQ value is 7.4. The bottle-nosed dolphin's is 5.6. The chimpanzee's EQ is 2.48, and the gorilla's is 1.76.

Bottle-nosed dolphins care for and teach their calves.

recovered in a sea park near Adelaide, Australia. She was not trained, but she watched trainers teach other dolphins to tail-walk. In this trick, dolphins jump backward out of the water and move backward on their tails. When Billie returned to her home in the Port River, Australia, she tail-walked and taught her companions how to do it. Wild dolphins are not known to tail-walk. Dolphins also solve problems and use tools. Australian scientists have watched dolphins use conch shells and sea-sponges to catch fish.

Dolphins are very social. Dolphins use clicks and whistles to communicate. They also easily learn to understand many human words. They are especially good at understanding hand and arm signals. Trainers often find that dolphins correctly follow commands using hand signals on the first try. In tests, dolphins given the request "right basket left Frisbee in" put the Frisbee on their left into the basket on their right.

5.6

EQ of the bottle-nosed dolphin, second only to humans (EQ 7.4).

- Dolphins are playful.
- They learn quickly and teach each other.
- They solve problems and use tools.
- Dolphins easily learn to understand human language.

4

CHIMPANZEES LEARN SIGN LANGUAGE

People used to think only humans were smart enough to use language. But a chimpanzee named Washoe learned to recognize more than 240 words of sign language. She could combine the words into sentences too. Another chimp learned more than 50 signs by watching other chimps. Some chimps even combine signs to make new words. One called watermelon a "drink fruit."

A pair of chimps and a pair of humans played the same video game. Players had to guess which move their partner

Mother chimpanzees care for their babies for several years.

would make before he made it. Chimps beat humans at this game. Chimpanzees can also remember the order and location of numbers flashed on a screen. Few people can do this.

Like humans, chimpanzees are mammals called primates. Primates walk upright and their eyes face forward. They have grasping hands and large brains. Chimpanzees show behavior very similar to humans. They live in families, take care of their babies for years, and work together. They make decisions and solve problems. Chimps are also aware of themselves. Like people, they recognize themselves in mirrors. They have individual personalities and can make simple tools. Chimps in Africa strip twigs to make food-gathering tools. A chimp pushes the tool into a termite mound. Termite mounds are huge dirt structures that can be up to 17 feet (5.2 m) tall. When the chimp pulls out the tool, it is covered with termites, and the chimp has a snack.

Chimpanzees use shells to scoop up water to drink.

240
Number of words understood by Washoe the chimpanzee.

- Chimpanzees use and understand sign language.
- They care for each other and are aware of themselves.
- Chimps can solve problems and make tools.
- Their behavior is similar to human behavior.

CROWS ARE SUPER PROBLEM SOLVERS

Crows may be the smartest birds. They are great at solving problems. A scientist at the University of Vermont studied the raven, a type of crow. He learned that ravens trick each other to make sure they get the most food. Adults feed in pairs and remain quiet to avoid attracting others. Young ravens make noise that attracts other young birds. This helps them compete with adults. A Swiss scientist watched a raven named Hugin trick another raven into checking empty food containers. Then Hugin sneaked off to raid full ones.

New Caledonian crows live on several small Pacific islands. They are expert toolmakers. Scientists tested some New Caledonian crows by floating food in a water-filled tube. The food was just below their reach. Scientists gave the crows objects that would sink and objects that would float. The crows dropped sinkable objects into the water. They did not drop any floating objects. This raised the water level so they could reach the food. In 2002, a captive New Caledonian crow bent a straight piece of wire to form a hook. He used the hook to pull a bucket of food from a tube. No one taught the crow to do this. He saw the food and figured out on his own how to get it.

Crows can be sneaky.

90

Percentage of buried nuts a Clark's nutcracker can find during the winter.

- Crows are expert problem solvers.
- Some crows can make tools.
- They have excellent memories.
- Crows are as smart as five-year-old children.

Some crows have amazing memories. The Clark's nutcracker, a North American crow, hides up to 30,000 nuts across 200 square miles (520 sq. km) in November each year. Over the next eight months, it finds 90 percent of them, even under snow. Researchers also learned that captured crows remember the face of the person that captured them. Even years later, they dive-bomb the captor and caw angrily.

The Clark's nutcracker uses its dagger-like bill to rip open pinecones.

CROW NUTCRACKERS

Some Japanese crows line up walnuts in traffic crossings. When the light changes, cars drive over the walnuts and crack their shells. When the light changes again, the crows retrieve the cracked walnuts. They get an easy meal by solving a problem. People have watched Japanese crows do this since 1990. People have also seen this behavior in California crows.

DOGS LEARN FROM THE PACK

People domesticated, or tamed, dogs from wild wolves. Wolves live in social groups called packs. They recognize and treat each pack member differently. Dogs become members of a human pack, or family. They accept a human as pack leader. They recognize faces and names of many humans. They feel love and jealousy. Dogs also love to play and "laugh." A dog's laugh does not sound like a human's. It is a breathy, forced pant. Scientists say dogs make these sounds during play and when they are excited. They also laugh to soothe other dogs that are stressed.

Dogs can learn to understand human speech and body language. They can fetch the right object when a person says its name, points to it, or looks at it. Some even fetch an object when shown a picture. Dogs learn best by watching other dogs or people. They might watch a person open a door.

Dogs quickly learn tricks, such as fetch.

1,022

Number of object names Chaser the border collie learned.

- Dogs live in social groups called packs.
- They can recognize both humans and objects.
- They can understand human speech and body language.

Then they open the door by copying the person's actions.

Dogs can learn the names of hundreds of objects. A border collie named Chaser learned to name 1,022 objects in three years. She understood groups. Chaser knew both balls and Frisbees were members of the "toy" group. Similar to dolphins, she understood the difference between words for objects and words for commands. Some scientists think all breeds of dogs can learn these things, but border collies are especially smart.

BRAINY DOGS

Veterinarians say the five smartest dog breeds include border collies, German shepherds, poodles, Australian shepherds, and golden retrievers. These dogs are experts in different things. Border collies and Australian shepherds herd animals. German shepherds are protectors. They often work with the police or military. Golden retrievers are hunters and loyal family dogs. Poodles have a great sense of humor. They love silly games, such as chasing and hiding, and they love to tease people and make them laugh.

Border collies are one of the smartest dog breeds.

ELEPHANTS CARE ABOUT OTHERS

Elephants mourn their dead. They stand quietly around a dead elephant for hours or days. Sometimes they bury the remains with branches and leaves. They also respond to living elephants in distress. They stroke, hug with their trunks, and make comforting sounds. They even care about other species. An elephant was trained to lift and lower a wooden post into a hole. He refused, until workers removed a dog sleeping in the hole.

Compassion, or concern for others, shows great intelligence.

Elephants form strong bonds. Mothers and young stay together for life. Related elephants care for each other's children. Separated elephants remember their bonds. Two elephants, Shirley and Jenny, once lived together in a circus.

Elephants stroke a dead elephant's body with their trunks.

They met again 20 years later and recognized each other immediately. Elephants recognize up to 100 individual elephant voices. They also recognize different human languages. Kenya's Maasai tribe kills wild elephants. One study revealed that when these elephants heard men speaking Maasai, they showed fear. But they did not fear people speaking Kamba, a different African language.

In the wild, elephants remember locations of water holes hundreds of miles apart. They also solve problems and use tools. When scientists placed fruit too high to reach, an elephant named Kandula found a large plastic cube. He used the cube as a stepstool to reach the fruit.

Elephants will travel many miles to find a water hole.

100
Number of individual elephant voices an elephant can recognize.

- Elephants mourn their dead and show compassion.
- Elephants form bonds for life and help each other.
- Elephants have excellent memories.
- Elephants recognize both elephant and human voices.

THINK ABOUT IT

Elephants mourn their dead. They also show concern for each other and for other kinds of animals. Explain how these behaviors show that elephants are intelligent.

OCTOPUSES FACE OFF WITH HUMANS

Octopuses and their squid cousins are invertebrates. They do not have backbones or skeletons. They have eight arms with many suckers, which they use to handle objects. The octopus brain is spread around its body. Each arm contains part of the brain.

An octopus's brain helps control its suckers.

Although octopus brains are very different from human brains, octopuses are excellent problem solvers. They are very curious and good at manipulating objects. A captive octopus will pull lab equipment into its aquarium, pull out drain plugs, and rip off wires. The smartest kind of octopus may

4

Number of years a giant Pacific octopus lives.

- Octopuses are invertebrates. They have eight arms with suckers.
- They are curious and excellent problem solvers.
- Octopuses are escape artists.
- In the wild, they use landmarks and learn by observing.

Some octopuses are smart enough to use shells to hide from predators.

be the giant Pacific octopus. Billye was a giant Pacific octopus living at the Seattle Aquarium. Scientists gave Billye a child proof bottle to play with. The first time, it took her less than one hour to open it. After that, she could open it in only five minutes.

Octopuses are also escape artists. Years ago, a British aquarium lost several fish before they figured out why. Every night, the aquarium octopus climbed into the next tank and ate one fish. Then he went back to his own tank.

In the wild, giant Pacific octopuses reach sizes up to 30 feet (9.1 m) across. They are usually 16 feet (5 m) across. They live up to four years. That is old for an octopus. They keep track of their location by using landmarks. Scientists think octopuses are the only invertebrates that learn by using their eyes to observe their environment. Some octopuses even seem to think ahead. Octopuses in Indonesia carry opened coconut shells across the sea floor. When there is danger, they hide inside the coconut shells.

PIGS: SMART, SOCIAL, AND CURIOUS

The pig is one farm animal that really knows how to think. They use their excellent memories to learn and recognize up to 30 other pigs. When one pig locates food, others find the food by watching that pig. But pigs can also trick each other to keep more food for themselves.

Wild pigs, called wild boars, first lived in Europe, Asia, and northern Africa. Approximately 20 wild boars live together in a group. This includes two or three females and their young. Mothers have strong bonds with their young. They carefully build large nests before the young are born.

Wild boars live in forests.

> Pigs communicate with other pigs using different sounds.

Sometimes they walk three to six miles (4.8 to 9.7 km) to find the best location. Mothers take care of their babies for two weeks before bringing them back to the group.

Domestic pigs are very social. They form groups and cooperate. They cuddle closely in their nests, and greet each other by rubbing snouts. Grunts, squeaks, and snorts mean different things. They may be warnings, show emotions, or signal what the pig intends to do. Pigs are curious. They learn tricks and routines very quickly. They even play simple video games, moving the joystick with their snouts.

30
Number of other pigs a pig can recognize.

- Domestic pigs came from wild boars.
- They form social groups and cooperate.
- Mother pigs care for their young.
- Pigs are curious and learn quickly.

RACCOONS ADAPT TO CITY LIFE

Raccoons are very curious and seem to play pranks. Some scientists think their behavior shows intelligence. Others think they might be using instinct. Raccoons do many things people do. They stand on their hind legs and use their front paws like hands. They grasp, turn doorknobs, open containers, and remove shoelaces. They can pick fruit from a tree and throw it. But unlike many smart animals, raccoons are not social. They do not form families or social groups.

Wild raccoons live in the woods. When hunted, they avoid capture by interrupting their scent trail. They run in a stream for a while, and then return to land. Or they climb a tree and jump from tree to tree. Then they return to the ground. Wild raccoons usually live approximately five years. In captivity, they can live up to 20 years.

Raccoons easily fit into city life. They sleep in chimneys and raid garbage cans for food. When surprised, they

Raccoons live alone.

run from sounds. But they do not run from flashlights. They do not see bright lights as a danger. They also do not avoid them. So, some of their smart behaviors may be instinct, not intelligence. But living in the city does make raccoons smarter. Cities offer many experiences. Raccoons' boldness and curiosity help them learn quickly and solve problems. They use trial-and-error learning. When trying to open a garbage can, they try new things until they find a method that works.

20

Age a raccoon can reach in captivity.

- Raccoons have grasping hands.
- They are very curious.
- They are not social.
- Raccoons use trial-and-error learning.

Raccoons living near cities have an easier time finding food.

RATS SAVE ONE ANOTHER

Rats are rodents, a common mammal with gnawing teeth. Most people think of rats as gross, disease-causing pests. They are surprised to find that rats are very smart and even show concern for each other. Scientists at the University of Chicago tested rats to see if they cared for each other. They trapped a rat in a container. They put the container in a cage with another rat. The free rat worked for a week until he opened the container and freed the trapped rat.

> A trapped rat will work to free itself or a cage mate.

ESCAPE ARTISTS

Scientists often study rats in research labs. The rats learn to run mazes and jump through hoops. In one study, scientists built a giant maze to see how well rats could solve problems. They tested how long it would take rats to escape from the maze. They thought it would take approximately three days. It only took a few minutes.

Rats are curious, but shy animals.

Usually rats get treats, such as chocolate chips, for learning a new task. This rat worked without treats. His only reward was freeing the trapped rat.

Rats have many behaviors that are similar to human behavior. They take care of their sick and injured. If left alone, they become depressed. They chatter when happy and make laughter sounds during play. They are very clean. They spend several hours a day grooming themselves and each other. Rats run from danger. They copy the behavior of those around them. Sometimes, they even eat food they do not like, if everyone else is eating it. They have excellent memories and never forget a route once they learn it.

1
Amount of time, in weeks, a rat worked to free a captive cage mate.

- Rats show concern for one another.
- Rats are curious but run from danger.
- They copy behaviors.
- They have excellent memories.
- Rats are excellent problem solvers.

SQUIRRELS FIGURE THINGS OUT

Squirrels quickly learn to do things they need to survive. They find food by watching other squirrels. They must survive all winter on nuts they find and store. They must remember where they put the nuts. Squirrels have excellent memories. They often bury nuts more than 328 feet (100 m) from where they found them. Squirrels also learn to recognize other squirrels as possible food thieves. They outsmart thieves by pretending to bury nuts or seeds.

Squirrels must remember the location of their food for months.

Squirrels are great problem solvers. Red squirrels can learn to open boxes. They try different methods to find one that works. They do not give up. Gray squirrels change their behavior to fit the situation. In a park, squirrels ignore people on a footpath who do not look directly at them. But when someone leaves the footpath or looks directly at a squirrel, the squirrel becomes alert and moves farther away, out of the person's range. Squirrels often figure out how to steal seed from bird feeders. Some homeowners make long, difficult paths for squirrels to follow in their backyards.

These paths lead to food. People enjoy watching the squirrels as they quickly figure out the paths.

Squirrels have adapted to cities and people. They may even think ahead and make plans. One squirrel wanted to cross a busy street. He waited near a crosswalk. When people started to cross the street, the squirrel crossed with them. Another squirrel wanted seeds from a pinecone. The squirrel carried the pinecone into the street so the car would run over it. When a car tire crushed a pinecone, the squirrel dodged traffic to eat the seeds.

Red squirrels are known for opening boxes and other objects.

328

Distance, in feet (100 m), a squirrel travels to bury nuts.

- Squirrels have excellent memories.
- They are great problem solvers.
- They have adapted to cities and people.
- Some squirrels may plan ahead.

THINK ABOUT IT

Do you think squirrels have types of intelligence similar to human intelligence? Which types of squirrel intelligence are most similar to human intelligence? Which types are least similar? Explain your choices.

FACT SHEET

- Instinct is present from birth and does not involve learning. Instinctive behavior is always the same. A spider building a web or a bird building a nest is using instinct. Intelligence involves learning. An animal that learns can change its behavior when the environment changes. It can learn from mistakes.

- Some intelligent animals do not have large brains. These animals include birds, which are also vertebrates. Birds have feathers and lay eggs. Crows and parrots are the smartest known birds. Not all smart animals are vertebrates. The octopus is a highly intelligent invertebrate.

- Many large-brained animals can use language. They learn words and ideas. They form sentences and carry on conversations. Apes communicate by sign language. Many animals, including dolphins and dogs, respond to hand signals. Some animals with small brains can also learn and use language. African gray parrots are a good example.

- Ants and bees are social insects. Each insect has a tiny brain, but when they all work together, the whole swarm shows intelligence. Herd animals, such as zebras and antelopes, also show swarm intelligence. Herding keeps most of them safe from predators. They keep their young in the center of the herd, where they are safest. Predators capture animals that cannot keep up with the herd.

- An animal's intelligence depends on its lifestyle. Squirrels and crows have excellent memories. They remember where they have buried thousands of nuts for winter. Many intelligent animals are predators. Predators must be smart to hunt and capture prey. Otherwise, they would starve. Octopuses may have developed high intelligence because they have no skeleton or shell to protect themselves. Intelligence helps them outsmart their predators.

GLOSSARY

compassion
The ability to care for others.

domesticated
Tamed to be able to live or work with humans.

instinct
Behavior an animal is born with.

intelligence
The ability to learn.

invertebrate
An animal that lacks a backbone.

mammal
A warm-blooded animal with hair or fur that gives birth to live young.

pheromone
A body chemical released by animals.

primate
A group of mammals that walk upright and have forward-facing eyes, large brains, and grasping hands.

rodent
A type of mammal with gnawing teeth.

swarm intelligence
A type of intelligence used by large groups living together.

vertebrate
An animal that has a backbone.

FOR MORE INFORMATION

Books

Fetty, Margaret. *Parrots*. New York: Bearport Publishing, 2006.

Gagne, Tammy. *Dolphins*. Minneapolis: ABDO Publishing, 2014.

Marrin, Albert. *Oh Rats! The Story of Rats and People*. New York: Dutton Children's Books, 2006.

Websites

Explorable: Animal Intelligence and Learning
www.explorable.com/animal-intelligence-and-learning

The Kids' Science Challenge: Animal Smarts!
www.kidsciencechallenge.com/year-four/as.php

PBS: How Smart Are Animals?
www.pbs.org/wgbh/nova/nature/how-smart-are-animals.html

INDEX

About the Author

Carol Hand grew up on a farm and has always had pets. She has a PhD in zoology with a specialty in ecology. She writes freelance science books—whenever possible about animals and the environment. Currently, she shares her home with four cats, all rescues.